Mom's Canoe

Mom's Canoe

Rebecca Foust

Texas Review Press
Huntsville, Texas

FIRST EDITION, 2008
Requests for permission to reproduce material from this
work should be sent to:

    Permissions
    Texas Review Press
    English Department
    Sam Houston State University
    Huntsville, TX 77341-2146

Acknowledgements:

These poems appeared or will appear in the following journals:

*Atlanta Review, Dos Passos Review, Flyway, Iodine Poetry
Journal, Margie/The American Journal of Poetry, Mudfish, Nimrod
International Journal, North American Review, Sow's Ear Poetry
Review, Spoon River Poetry Review, Taproot Literary Review,* and
The Texas Review.

Some of these poems were in the manuscript entitled *All that
Gorgeous, Pitiless Song,* a finalist in the 2007 Emily Dickinson First
Book Award (Poetry).

Cover Design, Lorna Stevens and Richard Lang. Cover Photo,
Robert J. Foust; restored by Schooner Stephenson and German
Herrera. Author photo, Donna Goldman.

Library of Congress Cataloging-in-Publication Data

Foust, Rebecca, 1957-
  Mom's canoe / Rebecca Foust.
    p. cm.
  ISBN-13: 978-1-933896-27-4 (pbk. : alk. paper)
  ISBN-10: 1-933896-27-2 (pbk. : alk. paper)
  1. Allegheny Mountains--Poetry. 2. Pennsylvania--Poetry. I.
Title.
  PS3606.O846M66 2008
  811'.6--dc22

                    2008049067

This book is dedicated to my parents: Barbara Redline Braim (1929-1999) and Robert James Foust (1923-1990)

Contents

Mom's Canoe

ALLEGHENY MOUNTAIN BOWL ✓

You can turn round and round and round
and always see mountains. Blue Knob,
Wopsononock, Brush, Davis and Lock
usurp the sky and conjure its seasons
—July's heavy wet sails, stars slung low

like lanterns, lily-thronged ditches down
in the cove. Winter's white bowl piles drift
upon drift, the air a thin gruel the men sip,
waiting for Blue Law Noon. Their coats
exhale wet wool and wood smoke,

their feet beat a work boot tattoo; laid off,
laid off, laid off, the mines mined out
and the Railroad dead, engines rusted to tracks.
Bitter cold at the root and bought too dear,   ✓
a hundred-year oak is two weeks' cordwood,

a doe, meat roped to the hood of your car.
Cinders and salt and snow turned black
and always the need to make rent. But don't
the trees wear fierce diadems after the ice storms,
and spring skies dawn fledge soft as new life,

over fields drenched in dew? There's the lark
in the morning, thrushes at dusk; sometimes
there are owls. Look at Wopsy and Brush
going dark, the sky's beautiful bruise.   ✓
These mountains calve memory from twilight; ✓

some nuance you knew once like breath comes back
with the questions   why the mountains come close
when it rains, what line divides false from true,
in what precise place do the mountains efface
into sky—indigo, violet, then blue?

STRIP MINE

A terrible, lunar beauty,
like leaves past withering;
when we run along the edges,
slag bits break loose and
roll down the wash
to the bottom,
pebbles round
as dark marbles,
bivalve halves of ancient clam
face each other
in frozen contemplation,
the animating spark
between, buried in sediment
eons ago.

At the edge
wild chicory
contributes its blue
to the green and white tangle
of Bindweed and Queen Anne's Lace,
then, the shallow mine pit,
wide, rusty gash,
obscene nakedness
of rock scoured of soil by the rains
since the miners packed up their rig
and left

this ledge with crumbling face
of limestone, gneiss, and shale.
Whole trays of layers separate
to reveal the delicate calligraphy
traced on slate, mystery
of ancient fern or fish
or link to man.

FOSSIL RECORD

Brachiopod, Trilobite,
Ammonite, Crinoid stem,
fern in stone with spores
strung like pearls along
each bract; snakeskin
tree bark, imprint wing
pressed and fanned; one
metatarsal wears a ring.

What has and what will,
pre- and post-virginal
virgin of be, preamble
and postscript of am.
Substrate less self,
negative space
embraced by stone
womb, Corpus Luteum.

Thick wedged slate,
old X-ray plates,
dense and dark,
shot through with light,
exposing heart,
the inner part of things—
what's been unveiled,
what's been enshrined

in sunken shaft
of mine or light,
bones thrown down
of Czar or thief
or bird or wife.

THE BEES ARE INSIDE ✓

We played TV tag under the tree, Casey
and me, screaming, scrambling away
from the bees. He tagged me out once

under its leaves then showed me his secret,
what he'd found on the tracks. He gave me
his best chunk of railroad glass, the size

of my fist; he gave me the Hope Diamond.
He had a face something fey, clear
as daylight in winter, too finely drawn.

How had he come from that stumbling line,
brawling and surly, dead-drunk by noon?
Not from his father those clear blue eyes,

not from his mother that hair like light;
Casey and kin were dawn and night, a bright
crystalline thing born out of darkness

and chaos. Inbred they called him and worse,
and sometimes he heard them. I saw
a cursed angel or changeling

flung headlong from God and then from a tree
we'd climbed a thousand times. It took
a purposeful, soaring fall,

the town whisper-buzz whispering like it had
for years, we kids not meant to hear
the rest, all that was twisted

and broken. Eyes clear blue, hair like light,
he said it all through the night

that he died. The bees, he said,
the bees are inside. The bees are in my head.

THINGS BURN DOWN ✓

My parents wouldn't come back for damask
napkins or oysters in frilly white shells.
If you understand, you won't have to ask

how Gramma knew linen—soiled, in the wash
she took in each week, or why she had to sell
baked goods in the street off "white trash damask,"

yesterday's newspaper. Papap hauled ash
or laid brick; he was skilled with a trowel
but there was no work, understand? Don't ask

what keeps a man from filling his flask
with what he'd divined from the wells he'd drilled
with his own hands, or why Dad's damask

was a gray square he hacked on to clear ash
from his throat. Thick smoke from the papermill
all day and night, understand? No one asked

in those days if that shit could kill you. As track
spread in congeries from the repair yards, fields
disappeared. Cinder and soot, more soot—damask

was work in that town. Mom found a dog lashed
to a tree, starved to bone. Too many mouths to feed,
do you understand that? She didn't ask

for much more than Sears Roebuck placemats
and babies that lived. What Dad loved was bells
and sirens, to watch things burn down. Damask

is not what would bring my folks back. I'd guess
garage sales, four-alarm fire bells, red squalls

of new babies, maybe a Bratwurst and beer

served on an unfolded *Altoona Mirror*. Not damask,
not fingerbowls for Christ's sake. If you don't
get it by now, don't ask.

(Villanelle variation)

ARCHEOLOGICAL RECORD ✓

Scotch straight-up, thy neighbor's
wife and Sunday Church
—Nobody's talking

but one white glove is lost.
What was said, and not. Gaps
outline the years laid down

in stone, but each wedged-in bit
is rocking. Dreams, cookbook
notes, the dress a mother wore

to a father's wake, or would
have worn—had she gone?
The shards meet to make

a pot you haven't seen before.
The walls are half-effaced,
but Zeus is raping some girl

somewhere, you know that
much. It's all here—battle,
faun, flush of dawn, grapes

twined into leafy crowns,
each loved thing lost, sieved
with bitter salt and ash.

THE DREAM ✓✓

My father dreamed all his life of a cruise:
sleek bandbox staterooms, turquoise water, hot light,
hints of unbound sex, indolent, spice-scented air,
platters piled high with pineappled shrimp.

He wore the right shoes when shopping at K-Mart,
bright white, and Panama Hats and Leisure Suits
in tropical hues. We all laughed but stopped after
he got sick, shivered, had night sweats, lost hair,

was drawn to bone in the stiff polyesters, head
magic-marker-mapped. He tried to hang on,
but lost ground, returned in his dreams to shivering
at Bastogne, shoveling lyme into Kauffering cattle cars,

to the year that taught him lust for every fresh-picked
ear of corn, red marigolds in a white plastic pot,
a salmon-pink blazer, life intact in the precise way
each fork was placed. When he got home

and felt safe, he began to dream big—exotic islands
under plumbago skies, winters with warm,
moist air, heaped platters and no trains
anywhere in sight. Until he got sick and learned

again how to long just for anything not broken,
and his dream-cruise diffused into the mere idea
of a voyage, or one someone else took, and then
he began to dream in earnest.

Light. Warmth. Food. Breath. Until he dreamed
himself dreaming a dream, then nothing.

ALLEGHENY COUNTY WINTER DAY

Ads for "Farmettes!"
in the morning edition
of the Altoona Mirror;
a single black buggy

sifts snow down
the back roads
past greenroofed houses
built solid with field stone,

outlasting the people
willing to live there.
Square white barns
in sparkle-stick fields

set at right angles
to the dark treeline.
Last night's snowfall
sunk under noon sun,

dull shine of whipped
egg whites. The old
Boyer Candy plant
has gone dark.

Day slants towards
dusk, the sound not
of birdsong but wings,
lifting up all-at-once

for late winter migration.
The six o'clock train
whistle bends its long,
hollow plaint round

the Horseshoe Curve
(the former eighth
wonder of the
engineered world).

Everyone's going
or gone. Sunset bleeds
through bare boughs;
snow hollows go blue.

FAMILY STORY

Mom talked about how when the x-ray
they used in those days before the ultrasound
confirmed she was pregnant the second time
with twins, she buttoned up her best
going-out dress, wondering what are those dark spots,
adjusted her hat and left. Weeks later it occurred to her
they were tears, wept for the long years behind
the long years ahead of diapers, glass bottles,
nights without sleep, no help with wailing kids
but from wailing kids. She wept
like she lived; when tears dripped and bloomed
on the gray wool of her dress, she looked up
at the changing room ceiling, expecting to find rain.

BACKWOODS

You'd go back to him, then,
your swaggering full-bird
second husband, fragged in Korea
and now hunkered down
here in this backwater?

How could you,
after he blackened
your eye,
dumb-bitched you
and wrecked your canoe?

You escaped from that place once,
his cottage collapsed
on the banks of that dirty, dredged ditch
he calls a river; all you needed was a car
where you could sleep, keep your things.

Yes, you're alone now we kids
are all grown,
but would you really go back
to that tarpaper shack
squatting in bottles and weeds,

where your beloved canoe still lies on its side
split like your lip
where he kicked it,
the night you ran home to us
in your nightgown and only one shoe.

BOOKS FOR THE BLIND

Blind from Diabetes,
Gramma sat in her
bentwood rocker
and tapped out her hours
on the front stoop.
She could get around
well enough to use
the bathroom,
pull on her hairnet
and support hose,
make coffee and fry up
scrapple for breakfast,
then move to the porch
to sip wind and weather,
drink liquid birdsong
and wait. My mom
mail-ordered the books
each week from
The Library of Congress,
lugged them up
the dirt path past
Gramma's old hand plough
subsiding to rust, to the
leaning white farmhouse
in need of new paint,
each book the weight
of a small child
or *damn greyhound bus*
hitched up on her hip.
Thick, flat plastic square,
like the hard-sided case
you might pack a bomb in,
all done up with buckles
and seatbelt-size straps.

Gramma's fingers frantic,
fumbling at the catch.

ONCE WAS A RIVER

His cottage down in the Cove
—mildew and wild roses,
thick vines choking

everything, outhouse,
grid bridge over sludge,
what once was a river.

The walkway exhumed
brick by brick from
sewage-soaked mud,

oak and elm limbs
locked up overhead,
old bottles

stuck into cinderblocks
under the joists. The gin
dumped down the drain

the day he woke up sober
by accident and saw
his lost history, the rusty

screen houred rest of his life
wrist-clamped to sad wicker,
rocking his terrible thirst.

combination of
~ emotion

FEAR

It was when I saw the words *Right to Life*
over disembodied,
stigmata-ed, prayer-knotted hands

in her waiting room, the Costco-size crucifix
above the desk
where she sat reading Mom's chart,

when she rolled the stone over the mouth
of any talk
about the need to not prolong pain; it was

then that I felt the cold speculum spoons
in the deep place,
felt the unfolding of stainless steel wings.

INDIAN PIPE ✓✓

Wild woodland flower found
only in leap year at midnight
in moss and fern fen. Rare,
lucent and cave dwelling fish.

Pale, cool glow, something
hothouse or orchid or mushroom
that melts at touch
or in too much sun—your skin

shift/transfer

is like that, thin membrane over
blue pulse, architecture of small bones
that build the body that
fostered five children.

I'm twice your size now, unrolling
blinds against the light, wrapping
you up in your blue flannel bathrobe;
so little of you left.

MOM'S CANOE

Do you remember your old canoe?
Wooden wide-bellied, tapered ends
made to slip through tight river bends
swiftly, like shadow.
Hull ribbed delicately, wing of bird,
skimming the water more glider than boat,
ponderous in portage, weightless afloat.
Frail origami, vessel of air,
wide shallow saucer suspended where
shallows met shadows near the old dam.
Remember how it glowed like honey in summer
rubbed with beeswax and turpentine
against leaks, cracks, weather and time.
All your housekeeping went into that canoe,
then you floated high, bow lifted,
arced up like flight, all magic, power,
evening light. You j-stroking,
side-slipping, eddying out, frugal
with movement, all without effort,
just like you walked and ran.
I still see you rising from water to sky,
paddle held high,
river drops limning its edge.
Brown diamonds catch the light as you lift, then dip.
Parting the current, you slip
silently through the evening shadows.
You, birdsong, watersong, slanting light,
following river bend, swallowed from sight.

ALTOONA TO ANYWHERE

Go ahead, aspire to transcend
your hardscrabble roots, bootstrap
the life you dream on,
escape the small-minded tyranny
of your small-minded Midwestern
coalmining town.

But when you've left it behind you
may find it still there, in your dreams,
your syntax, the smell of your hair,
its real smell, under the shampoo.
Beware DNA; it will out or be outed,
and you'll find yourself back
where you started, back home,
unable to refute the logic of blood and bone
you'll slip, and pick up Velveeta
instead of brie. It's inexorable.
Kansas one day will turn out to be Oz
and Oz Kansas,

with the same back porch weeping,
the same husbands sleeping around,
addiction, cancer, babies born wrong;
the same siren nights pierced
with stars seeping light, all that
gorgeous, pitiless song.

KINSHIP OF FLESH

I swung my legs up to the table
as I always like to do
and saw another pair
swing up, identical
gesture, length and curve.

I saw your taper-finger,
knot-vein, walnut-knuckle
hand just like Mom's
and mine, somehow
knitting together years
miles, dollars, cultures
of division.

Visits, letters, calls, e-mails
dwindled
until it seemed we had less
in common than people I met
in line at the post office.

Then you sat down next me,
sister, and I saw
what I had forgotten.

RAYSTOWN RIVER TROUT

It took my hook like kite-caught wind.
I had to fight to reel it in, to net
its taut dense-bodied surge, heft
and heave of oiled writhe.

I knew about the upstream mine—
uncapped and seeping mercury, so I
wore gloves to hold the fish no fool
would eat and waited for the mystery

and passion. There was no rainbow,
rainbow, rainbow, no communion
with Christ's flesh. Just this prism
flash gone gray and my wish

I'd never caught it; I wished I'd cut
the line before the glitter got away.

HOW THE FISH FEELS ⌄

hooked, jerked up from all
it knew; fluid, muted milieu
before bright bite of metal.

Gills burned, drowned in air;
under slanted blade, afraid
as rainbow armor scales away.

Laid wide open, butterflied;
broken-booked, spine revealed,
entrails tangled overboard.

Gutted, cut to bone
past pain or thought or
twitch of brain.

THE QUARRY

 We got there by following
the old railroad grade;
train tracks still glinting
under leaf-mold, curving away
through green tunnels
of old trees, low branches
sweeping us laughing
back down into the truck bed.

We broke through the woods
into clear shock of light
and rock scraped clean.
The old mineshaft walls
made a beaker of stone
holding an icy sluice
so deep that blue met black
in the center. No one had ever
touched bottom, all that
drowned equipment
and maybe miners,
with hands still frozen to rigs
and floating hair.

We shucked clothes, spread
towels on the limestone ledge
Mardi-Grased with broken
glass, Queen Anne's Lace,
paper scraps, and what
everyone there called
Blue-eyed Grass. We soaked
in the heat, air heavy
with fat, lolling bees;
blackberries steeped into wine.
Every year some fool fell

from the rocks, but we
climbed the highest cliff
and looked right down
to where the few scrub Bays
soaked their roots in the water
while the Jesus Bugs danced
a frantic Tarantella and the Mayflies
splurged their thirty days. ✓

CRICKETS AT LAKEMONT PARK

The crickets are sounding a catastrophe
outside my window, reminding me
of the painted tin clickers whose tongues

we'd arc and release, consolation prizes
for the perennially rigged ring toss,
that huge stuffed Orangutan getting more

moth-eaten every year, smell of sweat
and hot axel grease, gear eating gear when
the paint-peeling rolly coaster creaked

its way up and plunged past the carousel,
the real crickets' jig-chorus racket
in the long-limbed grass where we spread

our thin blanket. Then the carnival light
and crackle would fade, then I'd arc
and release again and again. Your hands,
your tongue, the cricket-sung, grass-sweet dark.

PERENNIAL ✓✓

When you've gone, it won't matter to the musk rose
twining the old trellis over the eaves. Willow
will continue to pour its yellow-green waterfall

next to forsythia, one half-tone better on the scale
of bright, and white jonquil spinnakers will sail
their acre of regatta

past hyssop's rising pale flower foam. It will
crest and subside and weave a sweet mat
to bear the thick blanket of snow

✓ and none of it matters. Not how you loved it, not
how you knelt in each dark December plot
to part the rich plait, reached

through the wither of winter to find something born
of the decay of all that was young once,
something still growing and green.

THE MOUNTAINS COME CLOSE WHEN IT RAINS ✓

Now she can see how the dull edge of a scaler
(when all you wanted was a few hours fishing)
could bring on a curse, how butchering a deer
could be elegy for life as it used to be,
simple, clear, in its way abundant—when a man's
family was hungry, he got them some meat.

And say it's ten below zero, skies gray so long you
forget what blue looks like, and you can't find a job.
Why not wait for the V.A. to open, your breath
hanging white sheets in the air? Easy for a girl
reading *Ivanhoe* to natter on about diademed branches
and fledged clouds over fields still frozen like iron

in April; she wasn't splitting the furnace wood; she
didn't have to clean out the well the summer it went
foul. A grain sack held four onyx-tipped deer legs,
each one sawed clean at the knee. Call it a prank,
hillbilly road rage. Here, the water doesn't taste of
bad meat or metal, but sometimes at night it glows,

warmed by a faint but distinct radioactive plume;
the fruit is perfect, but babies are blighted beyond
ken or control. Here, she spits her curses at traffic
and weeps when the oven shorts out the third time
that week. Outside, a bare nuance of season, one
backlit leaf against a dark bough. The underground

cistern is dry. Her arms bloom pansies, blue, purple
and brown. Winter's chill steals into her bones.
She longs for home, rusted rails going nowhere, fields
frozen in furrow and rut, paired mothwing tracks
that lead to the saltlick, tall hedgerow snowdrifts
in the high winter. Skies in a rainbow of yellows,

blues bleeding to violets, mine pits that open
their mouths to speak precise fossils. Boys who fly
from dark trees and precipice rocks and sometimes
survive. Spring betrays her green promise, fades
into fall. The whole falls apart, but still the shards
glitter, brown diamonds on water.

NOVEMBER

Gray and white
day after day
before snow,
old tintype
sepia tones.

Light muted
so that color
is an incident,
a jewel
that glows.

Sunset caught
roseate
behind
each web
of bare branches,

Bittersweet
wearing
brave motley
beside
the back roads.

The traffic
light is wanton,
an exotic
painted parrot
or harlot—

Emerald.
Burnt gold.
Then
throat-catching
scarlet.

Rebecca Foust

In 2007 Rebecca Foust's book *DARK CARD* won the Robert Phillips Poetry Chapbook Prize (Texas Review Press), and her full-length manuscript was a finalist for Poetry's Emily Dickinson First Book Award. A finalist in five competitions, a second chapbook, *MOM'S CANOE*, won the Robert Phillips Prize in 2008. Foust's recent poetry was nominated for two Pushcart Awards and appears or is forthcoming in *ATLANTA REVIEW, MARGIE, NORTH AMERICAN REVIEW, NIMROD, SPOON RIVER POETRY REVIEW*, and others.

motif —
things buried
and then unearthed